I think you're GONNA like this book.

LucAS THE DINOSAUR ENTREPRENEUR

WHAT DOES MONETIZE MEAN???

BY TIMMY BAUER AKA @AUTHORTIMMY

My name is Lucas,
and I want to own a company!

And be a boss!

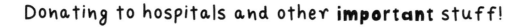

Writing dinosaur-sized **checks**,

Eating at fancy restaurants,

Having parties at my beach house...

Video game parties.

Donating to hospitals and other **important** stuff!

One problem.

I'm broke!

Ok, I'm not broke, broke. I have a **piggy bank** with 7 **dollars** in it... my birthday money.

How much do you have
in **your piggy bank**...

My dad says,
"You gotta make **money** to spend **money**."

Right.
Yes.
Of course, dad.

That's like saying "you gotta **make** breakfast **to eat** breakfast."

The **problem** is...
How do I make money?

Okay, this is going to take some **determination**.

"I'm 7 years old, and I think it's **high time** I figure out **how to** make some **money**!"

"Gary Vee-Lossa-Raptor, how do I **make** money?"

Figure out
what you already
love to do or already
know how to do and
MONETIZE it.

"what **in the world** does **monetize** mean?"

Ok first things first.
I'm going to **make** a **list** of everything I **love to do**.

And then see what I could **make money** doing.

Things I love

- Video games
- Cookies
- Cartoons
- TikTok

Ok. That's the stuff I love.

The other list is everything I already **do every day**:

Wake up

Go to School

Do homework

Play outside

"Hmm, I could probably put that one in the love list."

Bedtime reading

"That one is pretty good too."

"I think my head is going to **explode**!"

"Look at his **flabby** arms.
Look at his **giant belly**."

"I mean, he looks like he
could have a **heart attack**
any minute!"

"What do you suggest?"

"I **play outside** every day from 5pm to 7pm and 4 hours on Saturdays.

I could take **Toby** and give him plenty of exercise in that amount of time for say... 10 **dollars** a week?"

"Hmmm.."

"Take good care of him."

"Toby, I was able to buy this **frisbee** for you from **my piggy bank**, and it costs less than what **I'm making** this week!"

÷ WHAT IF... ÷

What if you made **YOUR** industry's FAVORITE kids book?

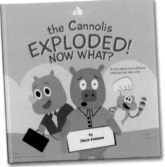

Let's make business less boring.
What if you created a kids book that your buyers read to their children every night?

They'll love it because it's about THEIR industry. And they'll love you for making it.

We ghost-write and illustrate your kids book in a matter of months. Kids laughter and addiction guarenteed.

Imagine having your customers asked every night by their kids to read a book that you made, that's about what mom or dad do for a living?

We want to help.   DinosaurHouse.com/publishing

At Dinosaur House...

Our mission is to create **EVERY** industry's favorite kids book.

You can find MORE Lucas the Dinosaur content on Instagram!

 @DinosaurEntrepreneur
(you can just search Lucas the Dinosaur in the search).

Or...

⁘ CHECK OUT ⁘

MONTHLYKIDSBOOK.COM

To get every Dinosaur House book in your inbox for free. Literally.

(we just want to build an audience of readers)

scan to get all of this

Go get **All** the books....

What are you **WAITING** for?

MonthlyKidsBook.com

12824402R00022